# Not *JUST* Your
# *Average Joe*

*Enjoy the "real".!*

*Chool*

## Joseph "Chool" Crawshaw
### (Amish for Joe)

ISBN 978-1-63874-147-3 (paperback)
ISBN 978-1-63874-148-0 (digital)

Christian Faith Publishing, Inc.
832 Park Avenue
Meadville, PA 16335
www.christianfaithpublishing.com

Printed in the United States of America

# DEDICATION

To my wife, Gloria. You have been by my side during all five of my books.

Your love, support, and ideas have encouraged me throughout the years to keep on writing. Thank you for humoring me throughout this process.

Well, my pencil point has broken, so this will end my adventure into the literary world. Glad to have had you by my side. I love doing life's adventures with you.

# CONTENTS

Please climb aboard for a trip down memory lane.

# CHAPTER 1

## *Personal Note*

# *Personal Note*

Before you read any further, let me explain that I am not comfortable writing the story of my life.

I am basically a very private person. Prior to this manuscript, I had written four other books published through Christian Faith Publishing regarding life at our bed and breakfast, which is located in the middle of Amish country. They were all short stories of the factual events that occurred at our B and B over the past twenty-three years.

I chose to follow a different path with this book. It is not only about my growing-up years, but also, I would like—as you read this book—to reflect on your own life growing up. I'll bet we have a lot in common on how our lives were molded by our families, friends, and others; most in good ways and some in "not-so-good ways."

I have always said that I am not a writer but a storyteller, so I would like to tell my life story by using the same format as my other books.

In a more "explicit description" of *Not **JUST** Your Average Joe*, I will tell my life story using short stories, experiences, interactions, feelings, fears, humor, tears, anger, hope, etc.

I hope you enjoy the read.

# CHAPTER 2

# *Setting the Stage*

# Setting the Stage

It was a foggy, humid early August morning. The sun was just peeking through the horizon. A car pulled up to the emergency room of our local hospital, and before my father had even shut off the car, Mother was on the gurney going through the hospital doors. It was time.

My brother and I had spent enough time in my mother's womb. After a contest of "rock, paper, scissors," my twin won, so he would come out first with me following after him.

Yes, unbeknownst to all involved, Mother was having twins. I was born approximately five minutes after my brother. You see, in 1948, the sonogram had not yet been developed. My parents had no clue, whatsoever, that their family had not only one but two more mouths to feed! A surprise to all! I had a big sister of twelve, a brother of ten, a brother of four, and now twins.

Which one is me?

# CHAPTER 3

## Home Life

# Home Life

Like most households of today's world, both parents worked hard to give us all a safe, healthy, and memorable childhood:

1.  They stressed hard work. We all had our own chores that had to be done daily.
2.  They stressed the importance of education. Homework was to be completed right after dinner every evening.
3.  Mother and Dad purchased their first television in 1958. We were allowed TV time immediately after school, before dinner. We loved *The Three Stooges, The Musketeers, The Mickey Mouse Club* (I was in love with Annette Funicello), cartoons, etc. But when dinner was ready, the television went off for the rest of the evening. We had to hit the "books." Our homework was then checked over by both parents for completion.
4.  Above all, all of us sat down for our family dinner around 5:30 PM each evening. No exceptions! It was preceded by a short blessing by either Dad or Mother (this varied a little when we reached teenage or high school years. We were all involved with so many activities, school, and jobs.)
5.  Sunday was church; Sunday school at 9:00 AM. Church at 10:30 AM, followed by a family dinner. All of us kids sang in the church choir and were involved in many church activities. It was an integral part of our upbringing.

I could go on and on telling about our early years growing up, but this isn't the reason for this book. Let me just say that all of us, prior to our preteen years, had a well-rounded, value-filled life. Our mother and father gave us a very strong foundation for our lives. That is what all parents should do (our culture has definitely changed throughout the years). However, not everything was fine and dandy going into the turbulent teenage years.

My old homestead.

# CHAPTER 4

## *Family Dynamics*

# Family Dynamics

My parents were indeed of meager means. Our father was a traveling meat salesman, selling meat to local neighborhood grocery stores, which were very common at that time in our country. Walmart and supermarket chains did not come upon the scene until years later.

On the weekend, Dad would work side jobs in his spare time. He was a butcher by trade and would work cutting meat in the family grocery stores through the community.

Our mother, when we were all young, spent 24-7 caring for all five children. She ran the household with tireless energy, like a well-greased machine. Each day, she would surprise us with a contest, a field trip, ice cream, crafts, reading, games, or a visit to Cold Stream Dam. Every day with her was an adventure. We all had a great life.

# Mother

Our mother carried a heavy burden all of her life. When she was three years old, she lost her mother. Her father was a severe alcoholic and died at the age of twenty-six, so she was raised by her mother's sister whom we called "Aunt Jane." We learned much later in life that our mother had a very traumatic experience while she was eight months pregnant with us twins.

With our father away and basically out of the picture, Mother was responsible for raising us siblings. (She did a tremendous job!)

Those young years were full of fun, excitement, laughter, and bonding, then the unpredictable happened. Tommy, our mother's firstborn and favorite son, died very suddenly of appendicitis at the age of ten. At the time, we twins were only two, my older brother was four, and our sister was twelve.

In those early years, if a family could not afford a funeral, the deceased was laid out for viewing in the home. One of the most bizarre experiences of my life was when our father took my twin and me by our hands and led us into our living room where Tommy was laid out on our couch. We were just two years old, but to this day, my twin and I still remember seeing Tommy on that couch. Neither of us had ever sat on that couch again.

After Tommy's funeral, mother drastically changed. The once loving, giving, kind woman who we all knew became a stranger! Laughter suddenly was gone from our household. It got so bad that a year after our brother's death, Mother was admitted to a "health" facility in our hometown. Aunt Jane was brought into our house to care of and to raise us.

Mother returned home approximately two years later. Aunt Jane was elderly and, because of some major health issues, simply could not take care of us children any longer. Mother was home for good. Everything was back to normal until our teenage years hit. Then, things got worse.

Still grieving from Tommy's death, Mother developed a harsh, demanding attitude toward raising us. Our sister, who had graduated from high school by this time, left home and got a job working for the FBI in Washington, DC. She very, very seldom came home for a visit. That left us twins and our older brother at home with Mother throughout our junior high and high school years.

Our mother, meanwhile, secured a position as town librarian, which was a forty-hour per week commitment. She blossomed in her new position and wondered if the loving mother that we knew in our early years come alive again. We all prayed for it to be.

Did it happen?

# Dad

When we entered our elementary and early junior high years, our father was promoted to district manager at his workplace. Although the extra money was greatly needed, his new position would require him to work away from home. Dad would leave home on Monday morning, and we would see him on Friday evening when he returned.

For the most part, our father was in and out of our lives during our teenage years because of him working away from home. When Dad wasn't at work, he would spend many nights going to the Masonic Lodge #3811 in our hometown. He was the Grand Master for many years for that organization.

Dad was a talented and dedicated fly fisherman. On weekends, he would take our older brother, who was eight at the time, to fishing streams around the state. Dad was well-known in the community as an expert fly fisherman. He taught our brother the skills of fly fishing. They were a pair.

It wasn't until later in our young lives that we had learned that Dad's father had been killed in a railroad accident in his early twenties. He left behind a wife and three children, all under the age of six. Our dad was the youngest.

Faced with a very difficult dilemma, Grandma opened her home up to boarders to make ends meet. This was the time of the Great Depression in America. Many of her boarders were men who worked on the local railroad. Hard work, with very frugal spending, got the young widow through the depression.

As I look at my father's relationship with me growing up, I can now understand my feelings when I was young.

I never had a relationship with Dad back then. I felt angry every time I saw him leaving on a fishing trip with my older brother beside him in the car. Let me explain.

As a young boy, I had been involved in sports from age seven to my junior year in high school. I wrestled in elementary, junior high, and two years in high school. I played baseball in Pony League, Little

League, Babe Ruth League, American Legion League, and one year in high school. I loved the sports, and I was fairly good at them.

Throughout all my wrestling matches and the many baseball games, in which I was a starter, I never saw my father in the stands to cheer me on. He never attended any of my athletic events! I would see many parents of my teammates cheering them on from the stands. When I was little, I always looked for my father, but I never saw him.

Oh well, maybe he was working? At least, that is what I told myself.

Many hours of playing baseball.

# CHAPTER 5

## Early Years

# *Early Years*

During our early years, we were never wanting for anything. Food on the table consisted of day-old bread from the community food bank and vegetables from our garden. Milk for us all was that awful; powdered milk combined with water. Once mixed, Mother tried to trick us by pouring the white "fake" milk into empty regular milk cartons. It was God-awful! We refused to drink it, so we had water.

Both Dad and Mother were very frugal with their finances. They both grew up through the Great Depression, nothing was wasted. They always had a house budget and did not deviate one penny over what was allotted.

That was great training for all of us kids, those were the fun years. I got some funny stories from those years.

# Baseball Story

Our family would be classified as low or middle class as far as income status. My parents would pinch every penny that they made just to make ends meet. As I started playing baseball at the age of seven, I was really excited; however, my baseball mitt had seen better days, and I really wanted and needed a new one. However, it was not in the family budget.

As I entered Little League, all the other boys had baseball spikes. I would have killed for a pair of spikes, then my luck changed. After a game, I noticed a player from the opposite team throw his spikes in the trash barrel behind the home plate at the end of a game. I waited until most of the people had left the stands, and I rooted through the trash barrel to grab the spikes.

When I got home, I was like a little kid in the candy shop. I had spikes just like the big boys; however, after examining the shoes, I realized why the boy threw them away; they were ripped and falling apart, but I still held onto them.

I rushed to our garage and used gray-colored duct tape to repair the toes, then dad had a spray can of black paint, and I gave the shoes a "new look." I was so proud of my new shoes. I didn't care that they didn't fit; I stuffed cloth in the toes, put them on, and just smiled. They looked brand new! (I wore size seven, and they were size nine, but I didn't care!)

When I was ten years old, I had saved some money which I earned from cutting grass, so I decided to go downtown to the sporting goods store. I laid away a brand-new mitt and new spikes. The owner of the shop wanted one dollar per week, and when the bill was paid in full, I could get the mitt and spikes. WOW!

However, I fortunately did not have to wait nor pay the bill. As I went to the store to pay my first dollar deposit, the clerk told me it wasn't necessary. He handed me my mitt and spikes and said, "Paid in full!"

It seems that someone that day, before I went into the store, had paid the bill in full with the stipulation not to disclose the name of the person to me. I am now seventy-two years old and don't have a clue who that generous someone was! I told no one of what had been done, not even my brothers or parents or coaches.

If that person reads this book, and if you are the one that made a ten-year-old boy's day, please call me...Play ball!

Amish Saying: Tomorrow's world will be shaped
by what we teach our children today.

# The Sunday Trip

Like all kids, we could not get enough ice cream. Ice cream was a treat to keep us in check. With Dad working away during the week, Mother would report if we were good or bad during his absence. If we were good, he would treat us all to an ice-cream cone at Howard Johnson's; they had twenty-six flavors!

So every Sunday, after church, we would load up the car, drive the thirty miles to Howard Johnson's, all the while arguing what was the best flavor of ice cream. Even before the car came to a halt, we kids were running into the store to get in line. The lines were long, very long.

After about twenty minutes, we finally made it up to the counter. We each ordered our favorite. Once I was in line ahead of my dad. I ordered, and then he told the girl behind the counter that he would take a vanilla. Vanilla! I could not believe my ears. I then said, "Dad, vanilla? Really? You could have gotten that at home, there are twenty-six flavors to choose from, and you get vanilla!"

Well, he calmly said that he liked vanilla. However, the flavor I got interested him. He made me switch cones with him. I got the stupid vanilla. With every lick of his cone, he remarked how good his double chocolate was.

I learned my lesson that Sunday afternoon. Keep your mouth shut, Joe, or you will get vanilla!

# Sweet Cushion Change

This story also has to do with ice cream. The local grocery store advertised caramel chocolate ice-cream cones for $0.25. After a lot of badgering, Dad gave us each a quarter for one cone. We couldn't wait to get the ice cream. It was good!

When we arrived back home, we asked Dad for another $0.25 for another cone. He said no—one cone was enough. My siblings were upset and started to cry. Dad would not budge—one was enough! I did not say anything, I had an Ace in the hole.

The "hole" that I am talking about was in Dad's pants pocket. Every time he laid back in his La-Z-Boy to watch a ballgame, his pocket change would end up underneath the seat cushion. My siblings did not know this. All I had to do was wait for Mother Nature to take her course. Soon enough, after ten minutes, Dad had to use the bathroom. I snuck into the living room, lifted his seat cushion, and *bonanza*! Four beautiful quarters were staring me in the face. I scooped them up and ran out the door headed for more ice cream.

I really enjoyed four more ice-cream cones which I licked hiding in the garage, away from my siblings. They had no clue until they read this book!

Sad ending to this story, I consumed too much ice cream, got sick, and threw up. At least the ice cream tasted good going down! Gross!

# Bucky

When I was in elementary school, I had two major problems, which were my curses with the kids in my class. I had a major speech problem, plus extremely protruding buck teeth. I got teased constantly by my classmates, especially by my twin brother. I hated going to school every day because young kids, as you know, can be brutal.

I was born with protruding teeth that affected my speech. A two-in-one curse labeled me with a new name among my friends: "Bucky."

At the age of eight, my father and older sister took me to see a prominent dentist in the area. His diagnosis was for me to get braces on my top and bottom teeth. He also recommended a speech therapist to work on my speech problems.

As I alluded to at the beginning of the book, we were a family with mega finances. When the dentist quoted us $1,000–2,000 for braces, I thought my father would fall off of his chair! Dad said, "What would plan B be?"

Plan B would be for me to play a musical instrument. The dentist recommended the saxophone because of the porcelain mouthpiece. By doing so, he felt confident that by biting down on the mouthpiece, the teeth would probably go back into my gumline. The cost of a used saxophone would be $100–200; well, within my father's budget. Hearing this plan B, my sister volunteered to purchase a used saxophone for me to try.

Problem one solved. Throughout the following years, my front teeth slowly but surely returned to my gum line. No more Bucky!

Problem number two was a bit more complicated. The school I attended for grades one through eight had a speech therapist on staff. Miss Thompson was her name, and she was not only gorgeous but also knew her stuff. She was a very well-respected professional in the school district. I loved going to her class. Ms. Thompson was my first love!

I met with Ms. Thompson three times a week for approximately two years. Slowly but surely, my speech improved, and my confidence level escalated. To graduate from the speech class, I was given a final oral exam. Try saying, "Sally sitting in a shoeshine shop, when she sits, she shines," without stumbling, three times fast, with no mistakes!

Finally, no more "Bucky" and no more speech embarrassment. I truly got a lease on life.

*Sidenotes*: As a principal, I have been asked many times to give a speech. To make sure I do not fall back into my bad speech patterns, I always get a good nap before I speak, and it works every time! Thank you, Ms. Thompson (I wonder where she is). And by the way, I still play the saxophone every chance I get! I made a lot of money playing that old sax.

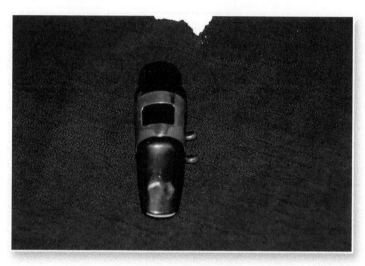

Notice teeth groove on the mouth piece.

# The Third Ear

Many of my young years growing up were sandwiched between World War II and the Korean War. Three young boys—my two brothers and I—were full of energy and mischief. To get us out of the house, my mother would say, "Go chase the Jeep!" What Jeep? You would say.

After the two wars mentioned above, the US government would give leftover Jeeps to municipalities to use at their own discretion; this is only part of the story.

Our house was located at the very edge of the town's open dump, the local sewage creek, and a massive swamp area. Mosquitoes ruled the entire area! To rid the area of them, the town placed a "fogger" on the back of the recycled Jeep, and every day, they would spray for mosquitoes. Sounds like a nice plan.

We listened to our mother, and every day, we would go out to chase the "fogger Jeep." Little did we know that the fog being sprayed was made up of DDT! (Back at that time, no one knew how dangerous DDT was.)

In the late '50s, we then learned the serious side effects of that chemical. All the young kids in our "fogger" group were terrified of the effects that they might experience.

My older brother and I had fun telling my twin of the ugly side effects. For years, my twin was terrified that he would grow a third ear. We checked him daily!

I can't believe that he believed us. However, we had fun tormenting him.

# Hole in the Wall

As you read in the previous story, many of our early years were spent tormenting my twin. My older brother and I would think of schemes to get him to cry. He always cried, then, of course, Mother would come to his rescue, and we would be put on time-out. My twin then would be laughing about our punishment.

One rainy day, all three of us were totally out of control. Since we could not go outside, we decided to chase each other around the dining room table. We were eight and six years old at this time. Finally, Mother was fed up with us and called for Dad to settle us down; that's when we heard his belt coming off. Run…run…run… flashed through our minds.

In our pursuit away from Dad, we needed a diversion to get his anger off us. Don't ask why—however, my older brother and I decided to shove my twin into the wall—head-first. I can still see him with his head inside the wall and his two legs dangling outside.

As planned, Dad focused his temper on him. My older brother and I, from up the stairs, watched as Dad paddled him. My twin couldn't move, and of course, he started crying. When Dad heard us laughing, he turned around and saw us at the top of the stairs. As he was coming up the stairs, we crawled under the bed.

Having a little bit of a stomach, we knew that Dad would not be able to reach us with his belt. All he said was, "Sooner or later, you two have to come out!" Decision time among brothers—who would crawl out first? We did rock paper scissors. Thank goodness, my brother lost, so he had to go out from under the bed first. I heard his cries.

I stayed under the bed for about two hours, hoping Dad would fall asleep and forget about me. My plan worked. I never did get the belt.

An Amish proverb is appropriate here.
As the Amish say, "Raising boys is like digesting iron."

# CHAPTER 6

# *Junior High Years*

# Junior High Years

Call it whatever you want, junior high years, middle school years, high school years. The education structure in our schools has evolved since the early fifties. For this section of the book, I'll call it the "junior high years" (tells you how old I am); grades seven, eight, and nine.

My twin brother and I, throughout our early years (grades one to six), were raised to be exactly alike. Our parents dressed us alike, and we were in the same classes throughout elementary school. We had the same friends, the same interests, the same hobbies, and the same expectations from our parents.

The junior high years are, without a doubt, where major changes in my life began to appear; where major conflicts with my parents became to surface and where I began to develop my own personality, much to the chagrin of my mother especially. I just wanted to be Joe, not just one of the twins.

At the age of thirteen or fourteen, I got the courage to confront my mother regarding the issues in the preceding paragraph. Not being in control, my mother was not a happy camper, nor was she receptive to my mother-son conversation. I sat her down and told her that I wanted my own life. I did not want to be like my twin. My demands were straightforward. I wanted to pick my own friends, wear clothes I wanted to wear, play the sports I wanted to play, date girls I wanted to, and investigate my own interests and hobbies. I stressed to her that I wanted my life to go a different path than what she wanted for me.

My demand list that was expressed at the start of my conversation with my mother brought out a deep, deep anger in her. She immediately stood up, gritted her teeth, pointed a finger in my face, and said, "They always said there was one evil twin." Of course, I couldn't keep my mouth shut, so I stood up, looked her in the face, and said, "Guilty as charged!" and left the room.

Little did I know that I had sealed my fate with my mother. We never had a mother-son relationship from that time on. The evil twin will pay the price for his new life.

The evil twin wants to tell some funny stories now!

My old junior high school—still in operation.

# Thumb up or Thumb Off?

All seventh-grade boys were forced to take a year of industrial arts (shop class) at school. The teacher for this class was a man by the name of Mr. Spotts who really should have been a prison guard or, actually, in prison! You pick one!

Mr. Spotts embodied everything a teacher should not do in the classroom. He degraded his students by calling us names, and he never uttered kind words. The glass, according to him, was always half empty. His negative approach to all of his students got him the reputation of the worst teacher in the school. It was evident that he was not a happy person.

There were twenty-seven boys in section 7-1, which was the highest academic class in seventh grade. We all had things in common. We each weighed around seventy pounds, we were all geeks, we all wore glasses, and we all *hated* shop class!

One Tuesday morning, Mr. Spotts yelled, "Okay, you dumb idiots, get your skinny butts over here around the table saw. This is the most dangerous saw in the shop. You idiots could lose a finger or a hand in a flash."

Picture this: Twenty-seven skinny, geeky boys wearing eye goggles that covered their entire faces just waiting for the class to be over—that was us. Mr. Spotts was still calling us dumb bells as he turned on the circular saw. Just as he started the saw, he briefly glanced down; that was his first mistake. In a flash, his right thumb went too close to the blade and was severed! There was blood flying everywhere, and of course, Mr. Spotts was in total shock. The machine was still running, and his thumb was spinning on the table of the machine.

Twenty-six out of the twenty-seven boys all gasped, except one. I calmly reached up and turned off the saw. I should have stopped there, but *oh no*! I uttered with a chuckle, "Well, Mr. Spotts, I would say your hitchhiking days are over!" (Maybe I should not have said that.) Vote one for yes or two for no.

Mr. Black, the junior principal, after I had just told him what I wrote above, suspended me for two days. OMG, my parents were going to ground me for life!

But I didn't care. I was the hero of the seventh grade for about a week!

After my two days of suspension was over, I had to return to school with my parents for a conference with Mr. Black. I was then sent back to class with specific directions to keep my mouth shut!

Mr. Spotts never looked at me. I got a *D* in the class, but who cares! I still had two thumbs to his one!

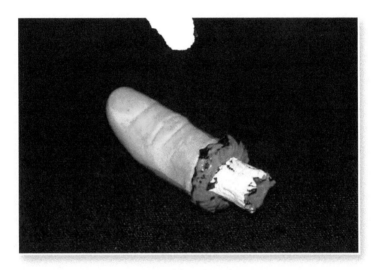

I saved his thumb.

# Behind Your Lip

Back in our area of the state, especially around the era of the '50s, chewing snuff among baseball players was considered to be a "Rite of Passage" to manhood. Many boys who played ball always had a thick bottom lip containing snuff. They even had spitting contests to get rid of tobacco juice. Gross!

If you were wondering—*no*—I did not have a big, fat bottom lip of snuff. I had a fat bottom lip of raisins. No one knew.

Being one of the oldest on the ball team, the younger players asked me why I never spit. I just told them that I swallowed the juice. "You've got to be tough to play this game," I told them. (By the way, raisin juice is good for you.)

Well, before one game, my coach called me over to the dugout. He asked, "Joe, did you tell the younger players that you swallowed tobacco juice?" I laughed. Well, it turned out that they all listened to me and swallowed the tobacco juice. They got very sick and vomited. Unfortunately, because of my "get tough" speech, we did not have enough players to field a team. We had to forfeit the game.

…Those younger players never swallowed again. In fact, most of them gave up chewing snuff.

…To this day, they never knew that the "tough guy" used raisins. I still love raisins.

# Crap Creek

In my early or middle teenage years, there were six neighborhood boys who always ran together. Once a week, we would meet and plot out our adventure for that week.

In a previous story, I told you how our neighborhood bordered a town dump, a swamp, and a sewage or "crap" creek, as we called it. In our weekly group meeting, we decided our adventure that week was to see who could jump over the crap creek. Do or Die!

In the early '50s, our town piped all the town's sewage to an open creek in the middle of the swamp. They were in the process of building a sewage plant, so we had to act fast before they got rid of the "Crap Creek."

The adventurous boys consisted of three neighborhood boys: my older brother, my twin, and me. Adrenalin was running high as we all got in line at the creek bed. Boy! Did it stink! What an adventure!

One by one, with all the rest of the group giving a verbal drum beat, we took turns making the leap. The first five leapers made it across with no problem. One had yet to go—my *twin*! He has great intellectual abilities (he is now a doctor) but no athletic abilities!

With verbal drum roll and cheering, my twin started running as fast as he could. He leaped at the edge of the creek. However, he did not jump out, he jumped straight up! Then, it happened.

He was in mid-air, directly over the creek. You guessed it! He came straight down, feet first, right in the middle of "Crap Creek." We all heard the sucking sound as he went waist-deep into you-know-what! I believe he was crying on the way down.

I have not seen anything funnier than what I have just described. We were all on the ground laughing hysterically while he cried. The laughing stopped after my older brother and I had to drag him out of the creek and take him home. Obviously, Mother gave my older brother and me a good paddling. She told us both to go to our rooms until our dad got home.

…To this day, the "Crap Creek Jump" will go down in neighborhood history!

# CHAPTER 7

# *High School Years*

# High School Years

If you remember earlier in my book, when I had the mother-son conversation about being my own person, instead of a carbon-copy of my twin, she had labeled me "the evil twin." I knew then that that conversation would come back to haunt me. I was thirteen at the time.

When I entered senior high school, I kept my interaction with my mother to a bare, bare minimum. I got into a busy life of after-school activities, band, sports, practices, church activities, and working two jobs. Basically, I stayed away from home as much as possible. I would remain at school after practice to do my homework. I worked, after school and practice, at an ice cream shop seven days a week. We would close at around 11:00 PM, and by the time we cleaned all the machines, I would be walking home (about two miles), arriving home around 1:30 AM. I then "tiptoed" up the stairs to my bedroom. I did this routine my entire three years of high school.

I enjoyed my life of no restrictions. I rarely ate dinner with the family. I even did my own wash. Mother, on some occasions, would voice her displease of my lifestyle, but I left her to vent her anger. After which, I calmly walked away. I wasn't going to "take the bait."

The only sad outcome of my new life was that I lost touch with my twin brother. We ran in different social circles, we had different friends, hobbies, and goals. The only thing we had in common was the school band, jazz band, and dance band. I was an extrovert, and he was an introvert. We were both very good students. John always wanted to be a doctor, and he studied extremely hard. Before we knew it, we were both seniors in high school and applying to colleges. Then it happened.

Our parents worked extremely hard to help us pursue a college education. John and I also saved everything we earned while working throughout high school. We needed to take the next steps. My brother decided to attend a state university to major in pre-medicine. Mother and Dad had other plans for me.

They wanted us both to go to the same college and room together. John would pursue medicine, and they decided that I could pursue dentistry! What! My "no restriction" life apparently came unraveled. I did not want to go to the same college as John. I did not want to room with him, and I surely did not want to go to be a dentist.

The underlying reasoning behind my parents' proposal was the cost. The school was a state university with low tuition, room and board, etc. Our parents were willing to pay for one year for both of us. Unfortunately, the college which I chose was a private, church-affiliated institution with costs at least double above the State University. I had saved enough for at least one semester.

My father looked at me and said, "If you do not agree with our proposal, then you can pay your own way through college." He then walked out of my room. I was in total shock. Throughout my four years of college, my parents gave me absolutely nothing toward my education. Nothing!

Needless to say, I was extremely bitter. I guess a major challenge faced me. How was I going to pay for four years!

…God provided each and every year while I was in college. Stay tuned for more information—film at eleven?

…Let's read some stories to change the subject.

# The Dance

My mother wasn't totally thrilled that I had a girlfriend as a sophomore. She tolerated my relationship with Carol and dismissed it as a teenage "Rite of Passage." She thought it would eventually go away. By the way, it did not. If anything, it got more involved.

Earlier in the book, I had mentioned that my father was Grand Master of our local Masonic temple. Every year, the organization hosted a celebration, which included a dinner and dance event; no formal attire, just suit-tie, etc.

As luck would have it, my girlfriend's father was also a Mason, and he, his wife, and daughter were also planning on attending the event. My mother was not aware of my good luck.

Carol and I hooked up immediately after arriving at the celebration. We spent the entire night dancing, laughing, and just totally enjoying ourselves. We were sad when the night was over. Great memories were made.

At the end of the evening, as Mother, Dad, and I arrived at our car in the parking lot, I held the car door open for mother. Then it happened, Mother was furious.

Without any warning whatsoever, my mother grabbed my tie, pulled me close to her, and with a clenched fist, slugged me in the face. My glasses went flying, I staggered backward with my mother still holding onto my tie, pulled me up, and attempted another hit. Then, my father yelled at her and told her to stop, she pushed me back.

As I sat in the back seat going home, I realized that my glasses were broken, and my upper lip was bleeding. When we arrived home, Mother acted as if nothing had happened.

…Lying in bed that night, I reflected on what had started out as an enjoyable evening had ended in disaster. However, despite the broken glasses and cut lip, I could still smell Carol's perfume on my shoulder. I smiled.

Photo of Town Square.

# Head on Table

It was the day before Thanksgiving of my sophomore year in high school. My parents were traveling to celebrate the holiday with our sister in Virginia. All three sons remained at home because of work obligations.

Mother had made our arrangements with our Aunt Melissa and Uncle Jim to have Thanksgiving dinner with them.

Early on Thanksgiving morning, I received a call from my girlfriend inviting me to celebrate Thanksgiving dinner with her and her family at their house. Of course, I jumped at the chance to spend an entire day with her. I had a great time.

The Friday after Thanksgiving, my parents returned from their visit with my sister. It was a Saturday morning, and I was having breakfast before leaving for work. My mother asked me how our dinner went with Aunt Melissa and Uncle Jim. I told her that Robert and John went, but I had dinner with Carol and her family. Then, it happened, Mother was furious.

My mother got behind me as I was eating and smashed my head on the breakfast table three times. When I was finally able to stand up, I pushed her away and literally ran out of the backdoor. I could not believe what had just happened. I had bruises on my forehead, and my glasses were broken, again.

Confused and in shock, I found myself entering the side door of our church. I had been very active in church activities and youth groups, and I had wanted a safe place to figure out what had just happened. It was only 6:00 AM.

I remember as I knelt at the altar and staring at the stained glass of Jesus behind it, tears started to flow. I was crying like a baby, asking God to help me deal with my mother. I do not remember how long I had been kneeling by the altar, but it seemed like a lifetime! I guess I was waiting for God to help me.

...I had to go to work, so I dried my eyes, put on a happy face, exited the church by the side door, and reported to work.

...I will never forget that day.

My Old Church—First Presbyterian Church

# The Turning Point

One of my two jobs while in high school was working as a clerk in a men's department store. One afternoon, my mother came into the store and wanted to purchase a birthday present for my father. I was working at the time doing store inventory, and my mother did not see me. My boss waited on her.

My boss then took the opportunity to tell my mother how pleased he was about me working there. He went on and on and on with many compliments about me. I heard his entire conversation with my mother, but he did not see me nor did he know that I was privy to his nice comments about me. I was fifteen. Then, it happened.

Without hesitation, my mother said, "Joe is just like his father, he won't amount to much either. He is just your average Joe. His twin is the rising star of the family."

I couldn't believe my ears. Did she really just say that? Talk about a hurt!

After her purchase, she walked out the door. My boss then saw me and knew that I had heard my mother's comments. I was in shock. My boss then sat me down and made me look straight into his eyes. With our eyes locked, he gave me the best advice of my life. He said, "Joe, you could make a positive or a negative about your mother's comment. You can feel sad that she thinks that and go into your shells, *or* you can make a positive out of the experience and prove her wrong by being the best you can and then rub it into her face."

And that is exactly what I did!

My sophomore, junior, and senior years in high school, I achieved in and out of the classroom, on and off the field. I had my A game going all three years. Yes, I did rub my accolades into my mother's face, but she never made a comment. And you know now, my mother's comments are the reason for this book title: *Not JUST Your Average Joe.*

I never told Dad about Mother's remarks about him; it would only hurt him. And to be clear, my twin was indeed a rising star… along with *his* twin, our older brother, and our sister. My parents did their job.

Another Amish Proverb:

"IF WE DO RIGHT EACH DAY, WE NEED
NEITHER BE AFRAID OF TOMORROW
NOR ASHAMED OF YESTERDAY."

# The Confrontation

"Turning Point" is only part of how I dealt with my mother and her comments about me and the physical abuse I suffered under her. Try this at the age of fifteen.

With a lot of prayer, I sat my mother down and told her that I overheard her comments to my boss. I then told her that our mother-son relationship was over. I wanted nothing to do with her. I wanted little contact with her. I do not want any advice from her, and I told her to stay out of my life. She gave me a blank stare.

I could not wait to get out of the house and get on with my life. Once in college, I never called home nor did I go home. When I did go home to my hometown, I stayed with my girlfriend's parents. My parents were not aware that I was even in town.

When my father drove me to college that first day, he parked the car, unpacked my luggage from the trunk, set them on the curb, walked to his car, and said, "Call us only if you are in the hospital." As he drove away, I yelled, "Love you too, Dad."

Dad did not want to deal with Mother's behavior. He did what Mother wanted. I believe he was basically afraid of her and how she would react if he did not do as she said. I truly believe he was glad I was out of the house. I was too.

…Little did I know, later in life, I would become closer than ever with both of my parents.

…Remember, honor your father and mother.

Amish Proverb:

"YOU CAN'T STUMBLE WHEN YOU
ARE ON YOUR KNEES."

# Just Call Me Doctor

This story, you are not going to believe! It was just an average October day at school during my sophomore year.

I was in my third-period gym class. There were dividing doors in the gym which separated the boys' class from the girls' class. That day, because of some reason, which escapes me at this point, we traded sides of the gym with the girls. The period bell rang, and we were dismissed to go to the locker room to get dressed and then report to our fourth period. As I was about to go down the stairs to the locker room, I heard my gym teacher, who was also my wrestling coach, yell, "Joe, you and Rich, get over here now!"

Coach was in the corner of the gym behind rolled-up wrestling mats. Also, behind the mats was a girl who seemed to be having a baby! Coach sent Rich to the office and the nurse's office to have them call for an ambulance ASAP.

Coach told me to kneel down and to hold her hand until the nurse or ambulance arrived, so I stroked her hair and tried to calm her down (I had seen that on TV); however, it was too late. The baby was coming. Coach seemed to have the situation well in hand (no pun intended).

I heard the baby cry, and I saw the ambulance pull up to the gym just in time. Coach and I were anxious to leave the scene in the hands of the professionals.

Walking down the stairs into the boys' locker room, Coach and I looked at each other and smiled. Just another day, another baby!

…Just call me doc. WOW!

# The French Kiss

It was my senior year in high school, two weeks before graduation. As I walked my girlfriend back to class, I kissed her on the cheek when we reached her classroom door. Then, it happened.

Unknown to us, the high school principal was behind us. He grabbed hold of us and made a big scene on the way to the office.

Once in the office, in front of about six secretaries, he informed us that we would both be suspended for one day for inappropriate behavior (kissing in the hallway). Carol started crying, and I was in disbelief. I was a top student in my class, two weeks away from graduation, and for him to make a big deal about the incident really set me off.

I then turned to him and said, "If you are going to suspend us for a peck on the cheek, I might as well make it worth it!" I grabbed Carol and, in front of the office secretaries and him, bent her backward and proceeded to lay a great big French kiss on her. She was still crying through the kiss while slapping me on the back.

The principal was furious, and then I heard him yell, "That will cost you three days of suspension!" The secretaries' laughter made him even angrier. "I am calling your dad and telling him how you behaved," he said, "you are out of here for three days, but not you, Carol." (She wasn't suspended at all! She enjoyed the kiss too, so why just me.)

Well, as you would too, I was in no hurry to get home. I tried to tiptoe into the house and sneak up the stairs. Then, I heard Dad yell, "Get in here now!"

Dad calmly told me that he had just talked with the principal and that he had told him the reason behind my three-day suspension. Then, Dad proceeded to tell me all the projects he wanted me to do around the house and yard that I had to complete in those three days.

Thinking that wasn't much of a punishment, I was anxious to get out of the door. Then, Dad also added, "And, Joe, by the way, the final punishment is that you have to double-date with your twin and his date to the prom." OMG! I would rather take a bullet! It would be faster and less painful. I knew that this punishment was nonnegotiable.

I grabbed the doorknob, mad about this punishment, and yanked the door open. Before I got out of the door, I heard my dad ask, "Joe, did you really French kiss Carol in front of all of the secretaries and the principal?" To which I responded, "Yes, I did." He then said the unthinkable, "That was cool." I was shocked! "Wow, Dad, you really are human."

We were both still smiling as I shut the door behind me.

I am still smiling.

# CHAPTER 8

# *Adult Years*

# *Adult Years*

As I now reflect on my life, I can see more clearly how various situations in the family unfolded! Growing up, especially in the early years, was indeed wonderful. We all were involved in one way or another in making our lives fun, exciting, interesting, and enjoyable! Then, it happened...

The turning point in the family structure definitely changed with the death of Tommy. Then, as we got older, our parents did not know how to deal with our teenage years. Our mother's lack of medical or mental treatment in Tommy's death was never resolved in closure. She became a bitter, angry woman. Medication and therapy would have helped her tremendously, but in the early '50s, there were very few treatment centers that dealt with the loss of a child.

Another issue that interfered with our family life was the decision to make the twins alike, dress, behavior, friends, interests; we had to do everything the same. Our parents could not understand that we had different personalities. We did not want to be the same. I did not want to be a carbon copy of my twin and vice versa.

This action, especially by our mother, created a third factor in our lives—favoritism. My twin was my mother's favorite. He did everything she wanted without any confrontation. That is the way he dealt with her, he basically smiled and did what she said.

On the other hand, I could not or would not, especially during my teenage years, live how our parents wanted to raise us. This, of course, caused extreme friction and confrontation, especially in junior and senior high school. As I alluded to earlier in my book, my mother became very hostile toward me—the "Rebel." I just wanted to be Joe. She never accepted that.

Most of this section is about our mother and her difficulties. Our father was basically not involved in our lives during our growing-up years. He gave Mother full control. He basically excluded himself from all dilemmas. He did his thing. I sincerely believe he was afraid to set Mother off. He realized that she definitely had problems coping after the death of Tommy and after the unexpected birth of twins at the age of forty-two. He did not want to upset the apple cart, so to speak.

Dad provided for the family, participated in community and church activities, and enjoyed his fishing. The only time he got involved with our lives was when we were in trouble or, should I say, when I was in trouble. Quote, "Why can't you be like your brothers!" I heard that a hundred times growing up.

That is beside the point. I was eighteen years of age at this time, and I am now faced with a major, major financial crisis in my life. Without the major financial support from home, I had to find more than one job to meet my financial obligation to the college.

Read on... You never would have guessed.

# Who Would Have Believed?

I would work twenty hours per week at the college kitchen cafeteria and my dormitory for about three years saving every single penny. On the semester breaks for Thanksgiving, Christmas, and Easter, I worked as a janitor's assistant cleaning and waxing the dormitory floors. On weekends, I would get a ride to my hometown, stay with my girlfriend's grandparents, and work at the two jobs that I had throughout high school—a men's clothing store and an ice cream shop.

However, the job that paid for most of my college years was definitely a miracle. Let me explain.

As I had mentioned earlier, at fourteen, I informed my parents of my desire to play sports in high school. They would not sign the sport release form unless I stayed in the band. I had to do both. Trust me, in 1963, no students played in the band and participated in sports. I look back at those years and my parents' insistence that I had to do both or no go, got me the best job I ever had, plus it was the most lucrative and most enjoyable.

At the end of my freshman year of college, with funds depleting quickly, the phone rang in my dormitory room. The stranger on the other line had received my name from a co-musician. They were looking for someone who played the saxophone, who would work on the weekends, who did not drink, and was willing to be a designated driver for a big band called the Blue Knights.

I could not believe my ears. It did not take me long to agree to the verbal contract, and before I knew it, I was the youngest member of a very good big band. I was nineteen at the time. The next youngest member was in his early sixties. We played gigs every weekend in Delaware, New Jersey, New York, and Pennsylvania. I learned so much about music. I was in my glory, and the pay wasn't bad either—forty dollars an hour!

Because my parents insisted that I had to remain in the band to be able to play sports, I was able to pay for three years of college with money left over. No more scrubbing floors or scraping dishes to make ends meet.

...To this day, I never miss the Lawrence Welk Show on PBS channel every Saturday night at 7:00 PM. I love big band music.

Amish Proverb: "You can tell when you are on the track. It is usually all uphill."

I still play the old sax.

## Just a Teacher

Harsh words hurt, and they continue to affect you long after they are spoken. However, as the years go by, one tends to forget or to hide or to dismiss the incident. As you get older, I guarantee that those incidents come back in force in your adult life. Let me give you an example.

I was thirty-two years old. I am ten years into my teaching career. I am doing what I love and, honestly, very good at it. Then, it happened…

However, deliberate or not at a family reunion, my mother crossed the line. Our Aunt Dorothy from Chicago attended our family reunion. My brothers and I had not seen her since we were very young. Mother gathered us around Aunt Dorothy and proceeded to tell her what each of us did for a living. Mother said:

"This is Robert. He graduated from the US Naval Academy, and he is now a commander in the Navy. He is in charge of many ships. This is John. One of the twins. He is now a very, very successful medical doctor with many other degrees under his belt, This is Joe. He is just a teacher."

I immediately had a flashback to my youth. Those words were not only degrading, but my mother's voice inflection gave a sign of disappointment in me. She looked at me, and I could tell she did not have a clue about what she had said or how she said the comment. Or did she?

At the age of thirty-two, and knowing my mother, I did not hesitate to respond. "Mother, without teachers, you wouldn't have naval commanders or medical doctors. I am very proud to be a teacher." I then politely excused myself from the conversation and went back to my table.

…I never got an apology from my mother. She had given me one last shot!

# Cutting the Forest

When I was about twenty-five years old, I moved back to my hometown to take care of my parents. I gave up my very lucrative job in a very prosperous area of the state to live in an area that I hated. My salary was less than half the salary that I was making at my last teaching job.

For thirteen years, I played the dutiful son's part. I accepted that responsibility. They say, "Honor thy father and thy mother." I hated every day with a smile on my face! I helped them in all ways possible.

I was a math teacher in a local high school. I coached football, wrestling, and baseball. In my spare time, I was going to graduate school for my Master's degree plus my Principal's certificate; needless to say, I was "burning the candle at both ends."

To add to my long days, my father, for some reason, decided that he wanted all the large trees, eleven of them, cut down in his front yard, split, hauled away, plus grass seed planted on top of that. My weekends for four months were indeed taxing.

Near the completion of the job, I overheard Mother asking my father if they should pay me for my hard work and long hours. I stopped working for a second to hear his response. Then, it happened.

Without any hesitation, my father said, "Why? I should charge *him* for the eighteen years that I supplied him with food, shelter, and clothing." Mother added, "I guess you are right." End of discussion.

I finished the landscaping project that evening, and as I drove away, I kept saying over and over, "I did the right thing, I did the right thing."

(I wouldn't have accepted the money from them even if they had offered it.)

# Anchors Away

When my father was in the Presbyterian Home and in his last final days, he was in and out of consciousness. I spent as much time as I could with him, but during the workday, a hospice nurse was assigned to his room until 5:30 PM.

Like I had mentioned, he passed away early one evening about one hour before I arrived in his room. The hospice nurse had called me. As I entered Dad's room, the nurse greeted me. She told me that she was finally glad to meet me because Dad talked about me constantly when he was in and out of consciousness.

"Your father told me that you are a Naval Commander and a great fly fisherman. You graduated from the Academy." The nurse went on and on repeating how Dad told her about all the ships I commanded, etc. "He said that he was extremely proud of you."

…When she was finished, I calmly told her that I was not the son that Dad was talking about. I told her that my name was Joe, and I am a teacher. She responded, "Oh, I am so sorry. I thought he only had one son."

…Enough said!

# Dr. Monzma

While at college, all freshmen were required to take the Old Testament and New Testament. I unfortunately was assigned to those classes at 8:00 AM every Tuesday, Thursday, and Saturday. The class ran for two hours on each of those days.

The professor was a man named Dr. Monzma. He was from the old school preaching "hell and brimstone." The best adjective from the class was Boring, Boring, Boring! I was a theology major at the time, and Dr. Monzma was the head of the Religion Department.

On a Saturday, about a month into the semester, Dr. Monzma passed back an exam that we had just recently taken. He gave all but one test back, and you guessed it! He kept mine and told me to see him in his office after class. Not a good sign.

I reported to his office as requested, and he immediately wanted to discuss my exam answers. Here was the dialogue:

Dr. Monzma—"I asked you to tell me how deep the Red Sea was, and you answered, 'It varies with the tide.'"

ME. "I don't see why I should memorize the depth of the Red Sea. It won't make me a better pastor."

DR. MONZMA. "Okay, I will give you credit for that answer." Then he pounded his desk with his fist and yelled, "Your next answer is totally unacceptable. I asked you to name three sons of Abraham, and you answered, 'Larry, Moe, and Curly.'"

ME. "Lighten up, Dr. M. Why should I memorize all of the children of Abraham? I can always look them up in the Bible."

DR. MONZMA. "I suggest that you, Mr. Crawshaw, change your major."

Well, it sounded like I burned that bridge, but I wasn't going down without the last word. I then suggested to Dr. M that he needed to lighten up. His approach of fear and domination in religion was turning many young men and women from going into the ministry. Religion is refreshing, positive, encouraging, and thought-provoking, etc. He eventually pointed at the door, and I got the hint.

…Now, let's flash forward to my senior year at college.

We were looking for a new advisor for our fraternity. I was in charge of the interviews, and guess who applied! Yes, Dr. Monzma. Of course, he remembered me from that time in his office. Then, it happened…

Dr. Monzma proceeded to thank me for my harsh words in his office when I was a freshman! He stated that after the shock, he began to rethink his approach to religion. He seemed totally honest with these comments.

We accepted him as our fraternity adviser. Dr. M and I became good friends. For the remainder of my senior year, he and his wife had me over for Sunday dinners. Who would have thought?

Larry, Moe, and Curly should take the credit for Dr. Monzma's transformation.

Amish Proverb: "If you think you are too small to make a difference, you haven't been in bed with a mosquito."

# The Visit

When I was teaching, I also coached the junior high wrestling team. It was our junior high match of the year. Two very disciplined wrestling teams faced off for the bragging rights of the area. The school gymnasium was full of parents, cheerleaders, and students from both sides. One could feel the excitement in the air!

My team was ready and anxious to enter the gym from our locker room. I was just about to give them the pregame pep talk when I got a word that I was needed up in the gymnasium.

As I entered the gym, there stood my mother and father. I stopped in my tracks. I could not believe my eyes. They actually came to a wrestling match! I was thirty-two at the time and never ever did they attend any athletic events that involved me as a participant or coach.

After my parents sat down in the bleachers, I headed down to the locker room for the pep talk. I couldn't do it. I was still in shock. I regrouped and told my young men that my parents, who had never attended athletic events in their life, were sitting in the bleachers. I asked them to wrestle their hearts out, not for the school, not for themselves, not for their parents, but for me. I wanted my parents to see what a great bunch of young men I had on the squad.

Long story short, we won the match, and afterward, each wrestler went to say "hello" to my parents. My mother and father were shocked, I was not. My parents left without saying goodbye, "Nice match, a great group of young men." I never asked them about their visit.

# Death of Parents

We could not take care of my mother at home as her Alzheimer's diagnosis progressed very rapidly. We had to place her in the Presbyterian Home in our town. It was a senior care center specifically for dementia and Alzheimer's patients.

My father would visit her daily and feed her lunch. I would stop on the way home from school and feed her dinner. This routine lasted for about six years. Then, it happened...

Our father, who was all his life a heavy, heavy smoker, developed lung cancer. The diagnosis was not good. He was given five weeks to live. Radiation and chemotherapy were recommended to help prolong his life.

After just one treatment, my father cried as he begged me not to put him through the treatment again. I did as he wished, much to the chagrin of some of my siblings. The disease progressed so fast that we eventually placed him in the Presbyterian Home too, right down the hall from my mother.

In the last week of my father's life, he would tell me stories of his life. He would ramble on and on until he fell asleep. He still, however, insisted on making the daily trip down the call to feed Mother her lunch. She had no clue that Dad was so ill.

Dad died on a Wednesday evening. The next day, I had to go tell my mother of Dad's passing. I asked Dr. Sullivan, Dad's doctor and our family friend, to go with me to give my mother the news.

Mother had not uttered a single word for at least four years. I went into her room, and before me was a very old, thin, sad-looking woman. I knelt down, grabbed both her hands, made her look me in the eyes, and before I had the chance, Mother said, "Dad is dead." How did she know! Dr. Sullivan could not believe what he had just heard. How did she know?

...After our father's death, Mother basically gave up. She passed a short while later. They are now together in Heaven, no doubt.

Mother, Dad, and Tommy at peace.

# CHAPTER 9

# *Conclusion*

# Honor or Love or Both

I believe I personally felt guilty only honoring my parents but not loving them. They provided me with food, shelter, and clothing. It was the love, the caring, the concern, and the pride that was missing throughout my teenage years. I never heard either parent say that they loved me or were proud of me.

However, I believe that God sent people into my life to fill the huge void in my heart. Coaches, teachers, coworkers, neighbors, all taught me not to ever give up. Because of their positive comments, accolades, and caring, I flourished academically, socially, and personally. I had my "A" game going all throughout high school and college. Nothing could stop me.

However, most importantly, these people listened and helped me plan my life. I will be forever thankful that our paths crossed.

...They showed me love. These individuals were my parents away from home.

# Anyway

Throughout my life, I have tried to live or to adapt to what transpired during my childhood years, school years, and finally, adult years.

I used the word to "adapt" in the last paragraph. One technique I used most frequently and quite successfully was humor. It was the sandwich effect. Humor—sadness—humor. As you just read, some of my stories were humorous in nature. You just witnessed the sandwich technique.

In my younger years, harsh words by individuals would roll off my back. However, when I got older, the words of others hurt me deeply. Those words would raise their ugly heads usually when I was tired, ill, sad, or quiet.

I was never one to confront or express my feelings to someone who deliberately meant to "word hurt" me; that was where I made my mistakes. I guess I was too nice.

The "niceness" in my no-response technique usually dealt with the comments of my immediate family. My mother, for example, would not hesitate, as you read throughout the book, to show her displeasure with me; both in words and, later, with physical abuse. That is where my dilemma of "honor your father and mother" came into effect. I did not want to disobey one of the Ten Commandments.

My meek demeanor with the fear of me hurting others was eliminated when I ran upon what I call my "Nine Commandments."

I came across a poem written by Kent M. Keith that changed my life. It is entitled "The Paradoxical Commandments," which I refer to as "Anyway." "Anyway" definitely had an impact on my life. No longer do I remain silent when others use harsh words. The sandwich effect is history. I never worry what other people think of me. I am what I am, take me or leave me!

The poem, which is to follow, is a staple in my approach to other people.

I believe that the "Nine Commandments" summarizes my philosophy on how to treat other people, especially those who disagree with me. I am committed to living my life under these parameters:

The town's library

The Paradoxical Commandments
Kent M. Keith

1.  People are illogical, unreasonable, and self-centered.
    *Love them anyway.*
2.  If you do good, people will accuse you of selfish ulterior motives.
    *Do good anyway.*
3.  If you are successful, you will win false friends and true enemies.
    *Succeed anyway.*
4.  The good you do today, will be forgotten tomorrow.
    *Do good anyway.*
5.  Honesty and frankness make you look vulnerable.
    *Be honest and frank anyway.*
6.  The biggest men and women with the biggest ideas can be shot down by the smallest men and women with the smallest ideas.
    *Think big anyway.*
7.  People favor underdogs but follow only top dogs.
    *Fight for a few underdogs anyway.*
8.  What you spend years building may be destroyed overnight.
    *Build anyway.*
9.  People really need help but may attack you if you do help them.
    *Help people anyway.*
10. Give the world the best you have and you'll get kicked in the teeth.
    *Give the world the best you have anyway.*

...Let me give you an example of the above commandments in action.

# Amish to the Rescue

Prior to Frogtown, I had been a high school principal in a local school district. I had a student by the name of Sean who had been suspended numerous times throughout his high school years. In the fall of his senior year, he was caught selling marijuana in the school building. This was a major, major incident.

I was well acquainted with Sean's parents from previous problems with the young man. They were extremely supportive of the school and had basically lost control of their son. After a ten-day out-of-school suspension, I had scheduled a meeting in my office with Sean and his parents.

We had exhausted all of our school's avenues to change Sean's behavior. His parents proposed an out-of-the-box suggestion to keep Sean in school so that he could graduate. One last try to save this young man—Amish to the rescue!

The plan was to reinstate Sean back in school, with all of his classes to run between 8:00 AM and 12:00 noon, he would immediately leave the school grounds and report to work at the Amish neighbor's farm. He would live with the Amish family. They basically adopted him. Any other school problems from Sean would terminate his high school career.

I never saw Sean in my office after that meeting. The Amish plan stressed hard work, back to the basics, and association with good Christian people. His old friends and bad influences had been totally eliminated from his life. By the time of graduation, Sean had become a very focused, polite, and hardworking young man. On graduation day, as I handed him his diploma, he hugged me and said, "Thanks, Mr. C." I told him that he should also thank his parents and his adopted Amish parents. Isn't love powerful?

The district had adopted a policy of "no tolerance" for cases involving drugs and alcohol. If I had followed that policy, I would have had to remove Sean from school.

I previously followed all the steps in the policy except the expulsion from school activities. The "out-of-the-box" suggestion by Sean's parents saved this young man.

Of course, I got a strict reprimand from the district office with a letter in my file for not being a "team player." Please review the "nine commandments" and then ask yourself if you would have done the same thing in Sean's case.

…The hug from Sean at graduation on stage when I handed him his diploma was well worth the district reprimand.

Local steers waiting for breakfast at Frogtown.

# CHAPTER 10

# *Reflections from the Author*

# *Reflections from the Author*

My first sentence of this book, basically, was a foreshadowing of what I was going to feel like when I wrote my last sentence. I was not comfortable when I decided to write this type of book and, even less comfortable, when I finished. Let me explain.

When I went back to my hometown to take some photos that you see throughout my manuscript, it was like reliving my youth. A flood of emotions—some good, some bad, and some indifferent—seemed to overwhelm me. I was definitely not prepared for the rerun of my life. Transparency of one's life only goes so far.

What you just finished reading is *not* the book that I had originally written. I did not like what I had read. This is the new, radically altered book but written by Joe the author and not by Joe, the angry son. The first book was not me. I read the first book over and over again and decided not to send it to my editor.

Our granddaughter, Sydney, typed most of the first book. I asked her, "What do you think of the book?" She then confirmed what had had me on edge these past few months. I was not a happy camper. Writing should be fun. I was not having fun.

The book you have in your hands was a joy to write. It deals with my life but from a different angle than my first book did. I do not like to remember dark days from my growing-up years, let alone put all those memories into print.

I am basically a half-full-glass-type individual. Now, when I read the new book, my glass is definitely filled to the top. I learned a very valuable lesson which, hopefully, some of you reading this book may want to use.

*Lesson: don't let your past dictate your future. Use it to motivate your future.*

I'm going to end this book by taking my own medicine. What is past is past. It is time to forget the "before" and focus on the "after".

I never thought that I could forgive, or more appropriately forget my early years growing up. I guess seeing my life written on paper was a real eye-opener!

...I think I'll take the first step:

Mother,

Maybe when I get to Heaven, we can have coffee together at the "GOD COFFEE SHOP". Then maybe, you'll get to know "NOT **JUST** YOUR AVERAGE JOE" a little bit better.

...Love you, Mother...

9 781638 741473